W0008959

CONTENTS

Fun Foods for Kids

When it comes to mealtimes, children can be rather fussy about certain foods and it's often the look of a meal that can put them off. Children love having fun, whether that be socializing with friends, riding their bicycles or watching their favourite film. And the fun doesn't stop when it comes to food! With a wide range of imaginative meal ideas and inspiration for even the most inexperienced of cooks, this easy-to-follow recipe book has you covered. Whatever you're cooking or eating with your children, make it a fun, enjoyable experience and bring the entertainment back into mealtimes!

GETTING YOUR CHILDREN INVOLVED

Sometimes it's easy to prepare and cook meals on your own and, with no distractions, it can make things a lot easier and quicker. But where's the fun in that? Children love to get involved and be nosy and this most definitely applies to cooking too.

Kids love the excitement of flipping pancakes, nibbling on ingredients, intently watching their cake rise in the oven or checking their dinner isn't burning! Set aside time in the day to make a meal with your family. Your children will love presenting their friends with the biscuits they created or will feel great pride in showing relatives the dinner you made together.

It is easy for us to clear the workspace in the kitchen without involving our children but you can easily get them involved in the preparation stages of cooking too. Write a list of the utensils and ingredients you will need to cook your meal and ask your children to tick it off like a checklist. This will help them realize how much time and organization goes into cooking on a daily basis.

It goes without saying that children should be observed by an adult at all times and a responsible adult should always be the one to chop with a sharp knife or put things in the oven. Establish these rules with your children prior to getting them involved and remind them about the rules while you're cooking with them too.

It's important to get children involved in cooking the recipes in this book. You can talk while you're cooking, getting to know why they don't like certain foods or ask about their favourite foods too. Knowing they have helped with the preparation and cooking of a meal will encourage your children to eat it.

BEING CREATIVE

Not only are the recipes in this cookery book easy and simple to follow but they are also great fun! It's a fantastic opportunity for you to be creative with your children and for them to let their imaginations flow.

The recipes can be adapted and if your children want to change the Bagel Boa Constrictor's shape or position the Happy Apple Aliens differently, let them! In the same way, if your children really don't like a particular ingredient in a recipe, offer them the chance to swap it for an alternative. It's important for them to have an opinion about the meal they're preparing and make it their own. This will give them a sense of ownership.

Don't forget to remind your children that things might not work out every time. If your biscuits burn or their pancakes are lumpy, they shouldn't be disheartened. This is all part of the creative process and more practice will help to give them more experience and improve their cooking techniques.

Children have such vast imaginations and – if making fun foods will encourage even the fussiest of eaters to enjoy mealtimes – this can only be a bonus!

BREAKFASTS

WISE OWL PANCAKES

MAKES: 12 PANCAKES

Preparation time: 20 minutes
Cooking time: 15 minutes

250 g / 9 oz / 1 2/3 cups plain (all-purpose) flour

2 tsp baking powder

2 large eggs

300 ml / 10 ½ fl. oz / 1 1/4 cups milk, whole

2 tbsp butter

2 bananas, sliced

24 blueberries, plus extra to serve

4 strawberries, sliced

75 g / 2 ½ oz / 1 cup flaked (slivered) almonds

- Mix the flour and baking powder in a bowl and make a well in the centre. Break in the eggs and pour in the milk then use a whisk to gradually incorporate all of the flour from around the outside.

- Melt the butter in a large frying pan then whisk it into the batter. Put the buttered frying pan back over a low heat.

- You will need a tablespoon of batter for each pancake and you should be able to cook four pancakes at a time in the frying pan. Spoon the batter into the pan and cook for 2 minutes or until small bubbles start to appear on the surface.

- Turn the pancakes over with a spatula and cook the other side until golden brown and cooked through. Transfer the pancakes to a low oven to keep warm while you repeat the process twice more to use up the rest of the batter.

- Top each pancake with two slices of banana for the eyes and use blueberries for the pupils.

- Make the wings and beak out of strawberry slices, then feather the owls' chests with flaked almonds.

FRUITY PENGUIN PORRIDGE

SERVES: 4

Preparation time: 10 minutes
Cooking time: 8 minutes

600 ml / 1 pint / 2 ½ cups milk, whole

125 g / 4 ½ oz / 1 1/4 cups rolled
porridge oats

2 tbsp runny honey

250 g / 9 oz / 1 2/3 cups blueberries

1-2 seedless clementines,
peeled and segmented

2 strawberries, hulled and halved

- Mix the milk with the oats in a saucepan, then stir over a medium heat until it starts to simmer.

- Add the honey and a pinch of salt then reduce the heat to its lowest setting and continue to stir for 5 minutes.

- Spoon the porridge into the centre of four plates and surround with the blueberries to make the shape of a penguin.

- Use clementine segments to make the feet and beaks then add a strawberry hat to each one.

PALM TREE ISLAND

SERVES: 1

Preparation time: 5 minutes

1 banana, peeled

1 kiwi fruit, peeled

1 clementine, peeled

- Cut the banana in half lengthways, then across into slices. Arrange on a plate to make two palm tree trunks.

- Cut the kiwi in half, then cut each half into six wedges and use to make the palm leaves.

- Separate the clementine into segments and arrange to form the sand on the island.

TASTY FRITTATA

SERVES: 2

Preparation time: 10 minutes
Cooking time: 12 minutes

4 large eggs

2 tbsp olive oil

2 tbsp tomato ketchup

7 chicken nuggets

4 slices cucumber, halved

- Preheat the grill to its highest setting.

- Gently beat the eggs in a jug to break up the yolks and season with salt and pepper.

- Heat the oil in an oven-proof non-stick frying pan and pour in the eggs. Cook over a gentle heat for 6 – 8 minutes. Meanwhile, cook the chicken nuggets according to the packet instructions.

- Put the frying pan under the grill to cook the top of the frittata for 3 – 4 minutes or until golden brown and just set.

- Slide the frittata onto a chopping board and cut it into quarters. Stack two quarters on each warm plate and squeeze a little tomato ketchup on top to make a smiley face.

- Cut the chicken nuggets in half and arrange to make the hair, then use cucumber slices for arms and legs.

KNICKERBOCKER PANCAKES

SERVES: 4

Preparation time: 20 minutes
Cooking time: 15 minutes

150 g / 5 ½ oz / 1 cup plain (all purpose) flour

1 large egg

325 ml / 11 ½ fl. oz / 1 1/3 cups milk, whole

1 tbsp butter

100 g / 3 ½ oz / 2/3 cup strawberries, chopped

2 bananas, sliced

100 g / 3 ½ oz / 2/3 cup strawberries, chopped

4 cocktail cherries

100 g / 3 ½ oz / ½ cup chocolate spread

- Sieve the flour into a bowl and make a well in the centre. Break in the egg and pour in the milk then use a whisk to gradually incorporate all of the flour from round the outside.

- Melt the butter in a non-stick frying pan then whisk it into the batter.

- Put the buttered frying pan back over a low heat. Add a small ladle of batter and swirl the pan to coat the bottom. When it starts to dry and curl up at the edges, turn the pancake over with a spatula and cook the other side until golden brown and cooked through.

- Transfer to a warm plate and repeat to make three more pancakes.

- Fold each pancake in half, then into three to make a cone shape and transfer to four warm plates. Arrange the fruit on top in stripes.

- Put the chocolate spread in a piping bag and pipe a waffle pattern onto each pancake cone.

KITTY CAT PORRIDGE

SERVES: 2

Preparation time: 5 minutes
Cooking time: 8 minutes

300 ml / 10 ½ fl. oz / 1 ¼ cups
milk, whole

60 g / 2 oz / 2/3 cup rolled
porridge oats

1 tbsp [caster] (superfine) sugar

4 slices banana

4 pomegranate seeds

2 blueberries

1 large strawberry

2 clementine segments

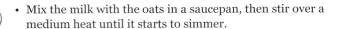

- Mix the milk with the oats in a saucepan, then stir over a medium heat until it starts to simmer.

- Add the sugar and a pinch of salt then reduce the heat to its lowest setting and continue to stir for 5 minutes.

- Divide the porridge between two warm bowls and make the eyes from banana and pomegranate. Add blueberry noses.

- Slice the strawberries, then cut each slice into thin strips to make the whiskers. Complete the faces with clementine smiles.

FRUIT BOWL BIRDY

SERVES: 1

Preparation time: 10 minutes

1 Granny Smith apple

1 kiwi fruit

1 wedge pink grapefruit

1 red grape

2 blueberries

- Cut the apple in half and use a melon baller to remove the core. Cut a third off one of the halves, then cut a beak and the lower legs out of it.

- Cut four thick slices of kiwi. Cut one of the slices into three strips to use for the neck and upper legs.

- Cut the grape in half then cut one of the halves in half again for the feet. Cut two slices from the other half for the eyes.

- Assemble all the pieces on a plate and add blueberries to the eyes for the pupils.

PROUD LION PANCAKES

SERVES: 4

Preparation time: 20 minutes
Cooking time: 10 minutes

125 g / 4 ½ oz / ¾ cup plain
(all-purpose) flour

1 tsp baking powder

1 large egg, beaten

150 ml / 5 ½ fl. oz / 2/3 cup
milk, whole

1 tbsp butter

150 g / 5 ½ oz / 1 cup
strawberries, sliced

1 large carrot, peeled and julienned

5 apricots, halved and stoned

4 raspberries

8 blueberries

runny honey and Greek yogurt
to serve

- Mix the flour and baking powder in a bowl, then whisk in the egg and milk until smooth.

- Melt the butter in a frying pan then whisk it into the batter. Put the buttered frying pan back over a low heat.

- You will need a tablespoon of batter for each pancake and you should be able to cook four pancakes at a time in the frying pan. Spoon the batter into the pan and cook for 2 minutes or until small bubbles start to appear on the surface.

- Turn the pancakes over with a spatula and cook the other side until golden brown. Keep the pancakes warm in a low oven while you repeat the process with the rest of the mixture.

- Stack two pancakes on each plate and make the mane from strawberry slices and julienned carrot. Cut one of the apricots into eight wedges and position for the eyebrows and use the rest of the fruit to make the face.

- Serve with honey and yogurt for spooning over at the table.

NUTTY BUTTER BEARS

MAKES: 2

Preparation time: 10 minutes

2 slices granary bread

2 tbsp smooth peanut butter

2 tbsp dulce de leche

6 slices banana

6 raisins

• Toast the bread in a toaster or under a hot grill.

• Mix the peanut butter with the dulce de leche, then spread it on top of the hot toast.

• Lay three banana slices on top of each piece of toast to make the ears and muzzles, then raisins for the eyes and noses.

SUNNY-SIDE UP SANDWICH

SERVES: 1

Preparation time: 5 minutes
Cooking time: 8 minutes

2 slices white bread

1 slice Manchego

1 tbsp sunflower oil

1 large egg

½ boiled carrot, julienned

2 slices black olive

2 small pieces mild red chilli

- Preheat the grill to medium, then toast the bread on one side. Turn the bread over, top one slice with cheese and toast until the toast is golden and the cheese has melted.

- Meanwhile, heat the sunflower oil in a frying pan then fry the egg over a low heat until the white sets.

- Put the plain toast on a plate and top with the grilled cheese toast. Lay the egg on top and arrange the carrot round the outside of the yolk to form the sun's rays. Make a face from the olive and chilli slices.

BANANA BASS
BREAKFAST PANCAKES

SERVES: 6

Preparation time: 20 minutes
Cooking time: 15 minutes

250 g / 9 oz / 1 2/3 cups plain (all-purpose) flour

2 tsp baking powder

2 large eggs, beaten

300 ml / 10 ½ fl. oz / 1 1/4 cups milk, whole

2 tbsp butter

75 g / 2 ½ oz / 1/3 cup smooth peanut butter

3 bananas, sliced

2 seedless clementines, peeled and segmented

150 g / 5 ½ oz / 1 cup blueberries

3 kiwi fruit, peeled and sliced

- Mix the flour and baking powder in a bowl, then whisk in the eggs and milk until smooth.

- Melt the butter in a large frying pan then whisk it into the batter. Put the buttered frying pan back over a low heat.

- You will need a tablespoon of batter for each pancake and you should be able to cook four pancakes at a time in the frying pan. Spoon the batter into the pan and cook for 2 minutes or until small bubbles start to appear on the surface.

- Turn the pancakes over with a spatula and cook the other side until golden brown. Keep the pancakes warm in a low oven while you repeat the process twice more.

- Sandwich the pancakes together in pairs with the peanut butter and arrange the banana slices on top to make scales.

- Make the fish fins, tails and lips from clementine segments. Halve three of the blueberries to use as eyes, then use the rest to form bubbles.

- Cut the kiwi slices into ribbons, leaving a small strip at the base intact to keep them together, then position as seaweed at the bottom of the plates.

LUNCH

Sailboat Bruschetta

MAKES: 8 BOATS

Preparation time: 15 minutes

2 thick slices honey-roast ham

8 slices wholemeal baguette

2 small tomatoes, quartered

8 basil leaves

4 cheese slices, halved diagonally

- Cut the ham into pieces and arrange on top of the baguette slices.

- Top each one with a piece of tomato and a basil leaf.

- Use a flag-topped cocktail stick to skewer each cheese triangle, then insert into the top of the bruschetta to hold everything in place.

SOUP WITH A SMILE

SERVES: 4

Preparation time: 10 minutes
Cooking time: 30 minutes

2 tbsp olive oil

2 tbsp butter

1 leek, chopped

2 cloves of garlic, crushed

2 carrots, chopped

1 large potato, cubed

2 courgettes (zucchini), chopped

1 litre / 1 pint 15 fl. oz / 4 cups
vegetable stock

4 tbsp double cream

8 thin slices baguette, white

- Heat the oil and butter in a saucepan and fry the leeks for 8 minutes or until softened.

- Add the garlic and the rest of the vegetables to the pan and cook for 2 more minutes, then stir in the vegetable stock and bring to the boil.

- Simmer for 20 minutes then blend in a food processor or liquidiser until smooth. Taste the soup for seasoning and add salt and pepper as necessary.

- Ladle the soup into warm bowls and drizzle the cream on top to make a smiley face. Add baguette slices for ears and serve immediately.

Egg Mayo Monsters

MAKES: 2

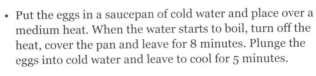

Preparation time: 20 minutes
Cooking time: 15 minutes

3 large eggs

50 ml / 1 ¾ fl. oz / ¼ cup mayonnaise

¼ red onion, finely chopped

2 tbsp canned sweetcorn

1 tbsp chives, chopped

2 slices toast

1 tomato, halved

1 slice yellow pepper

1 slice gherkin

½ carrot, peeled

1 slice green pepper

2 slices black olive

- Put the eggs in a saucepan of cold water and place over a medium heat. When the water starts to boil, turn off the heat, cover the pan and leave for 8 minutes. Plunge the eggs into cold water and leave to cool for 5 minutes.

- Drain and peel the eggs. Cut two slices from the centre of one of the eggs and set aside, then mash the rest roughly with a fork. Stir in the mayonnaise, onion, sweetcorn and chives and season to taste with salt and pepper.

- Spread the egg mayonnaise over the toast. Top one piece with the reserved egg slices to make eyes and use the tomatoes for pupils. Cut a small piece off the end of the yellow pepper slice and use the rest for the smile, adding a gherkin nose.

- Cut a few whiskers from the carrot, then grate the rest and use as the hair for the second slice. Use the reserved piece of yellow pepper for the nose, a green pepper smile and black olive eyes.

FISH BOWL BUTTIES

SERVES: 4

Preparation time: 10 minutes

2 tbsp butter, softened

8 slices wholemeal toast,
crusts removed

12 slices salami

2 cooked carrots, 1 sliced and 1 diced

8 cooked green beans, cut into
short lengths

a handful cooked peas

4 slices cucumber, halved

4 slices black olive

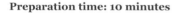

- Butter the toast and make it into four sandwiches with the salami.

- Top each sandwich 'fish' with scales make from halved slices of carrot, then add an extra slice for the eyes and top with pieces of olive.

- Create the sea bed with diced carrot and pieces of green bean, then add pea 'bubbles'. Complete the fish with cucumber tails.

35

TEATIME TIPI

SERVES: 1

Preparation time: 10 minutes

4 slices white bread

1 tbsp butter, softened

1 slice ham

1 slice cheese

2 pretzel sticks

3 slices cucumber

½ cherry tomato

6 hoop crisps

- Spread the bread with butter and make two of the slices into a ham sandwich and two of the slices into a cheese sandwich. Cut off the crusts then cut each one into two triangles.

- Arrange the sandwiches in a pyramid shape, using pretzel sticks for the tent poles.

- Make a door flap from the cucumber and tomato and surround the tipi with potato hoops.

BAGEL BOA CONSTRICTOR

MAKES: 2

Preparation time: 20 minutes

3 wholemeal bagels

2 tbsp butter, softened

1 hard-boiled egg, chopped

1 tbsp cress

3 slices ham

75 g / 2 ½ oz / 0.75 cup Cheddar, cut into small pieces

1 cherry tomato, sliced

75 g / 2 ½ oz / 1/3 cup canned tuna, drained and flaked

1 tbsp canned sweetcorn

1 tbsp cucumber, diced

2 mini waxed cheeses, wax removed and sliced

6 blueberries

1 finger roll, halved

2 stuffed green olives, sliced

4 chives

- Halve the bagels horizontally and toast under a hot grill or in a toaster. Spread with butter, then cut each one in half and arrange on two serving plates in the shape of a snake.

- Top the first two halves with chopped egg and cress. Stack the ham slices, then roll them up and cut the roll into ten slices. Arrange on top of the next two bagel halves.

- Top the following halves with Cheddar and tomato, then spread the next ones with tuna and garnish with sweetcorn and cucumber.

- Arrange the mini waxed cheese slices on the final bagel half and garnish with blueberries. Complete each snake with a finger roll head, olive eyes and a chive tongue.

SALAMI SANDWICH

MAKES: 1

Preparation time: 15 minutes

2 slices white bread

1 tbsp cream cheese

1 slice Cheddar cheese

1 lettuce leaf

1 large slice salami

2 slices garlic sausage

1 green olive, halved

1 black olive, halved

½ cherry tomato

4 pretzel sticks

- Spread the bread with cream cheese and top one of the slices with Cheddar, then transfer it to a lettuce lined plate.

- Top the second slice of bread with salami and trim to fit. Cut a slice off the right hand side of the bread starting a third of the way towards the centre at the top, and tapering towards the bottom corner. Repeat on the other side. Flip the central piece over and lay it on top of the cheese. Turn the two outside pieces 180° to form the ears.

- Top the garlic sausage slices with green olive halves to make the eyes and cut one of the black olive halves into two discs for the pupils. Use the other black olive half for the nose.

- Use the salami off-cuts to make a tail then complete the dog with a pickled plum tongue and pretzel stick legs.

BLOOMING SALAD BAPS

SERVES: 2

Preparation time: 15 minutes

2 sesame and rye baps

2 tbsp cream cheese

¼ cucumber, sliced

3 tomatoes

50 g / 1 ¾ oz / 1/3 cup canned sweetcorn

1 chive, cut into short lengths

2 cooked peas

- Cut the baps in half horizontally and spread them with cream cheese.

- Put the bases on two plates and arrange a few slices on cucumber on top of each to form the leaves. Lay the other half of the baps on top with the cream cheese uppermost.

- Cut each tomato into 10 wedges and arrange on top to make the petals of the flower.

- Make the centre of the blooms from sweetcorn, chives and peas.

OUTER SPACE SANDWICH

SERVES: 4

Preparation time: 20 minutes
Cooking time: 5 minutes

3 large eggs, beaten

1 tbsp butter

4 slices white bread

2 tbsp butter, softened

8 slices mortadella

4 slices Leerdammer cheese

4 slices Red Leicester cheese

¼ sheet nori seaweed

12 slices pepperoni

star-shaped savoury snacks to garnish

- Season the beaten eggs with salt and pepper. Melt the butter in a large frying pan, then pour in the eggs and cook over a medium heat until the egg is set on top. Turn the omelette out onto a chopping board and leave to cool a little.

- Meanwhile, spread the bread with butter and top with mortadella, cutting the slices to fit if necessary.

- Use a large round cookie cutter to cut the Leerdammer slices into moon-shapes, then use a star-shaped cookie cutter to cut stars out of the off-cuts. Arrange on top of the mortadella.

- Use a gingerbread man cutter to cut four astronauts out of the Red Leicester, then use scissors to cut visors out of the nori.

- Use a space rocket cutter to cut four pieces of omelette and add pepperoni portholes. Garnish the plates with star-shaped snacks before serving.

TOMMY TOMATO SOUP

SERVES: 4

Preparation time: 15 minutes
Cooking time: 30 minutes

2 tbsp olive oil

1 onion, finely chopped

4 cloves of garlic, crushed

450 g / 1 lb ripe / 3 cups ripe
tomatoes, diced

500 ml / 17 ½ fl. oz / 2 cups
vegetable stock

8 basil leaves

8 slices black olive

150 g / 5 ½ oz / 2/3 cup
cream cheese

grissini to serve

- Heat the oil in a saucepan and fry the onion for 8 minutes or until softened. Add the garlic to the pan and cook for 2 minutes, then stir in the tomatoes and vegetable stock.

- Simmer for 20 minutes then blend until smooth with a liquidiser or immersion blender.

- Taste the soup and adjust the seasoning with salt and pepper, then ladle into four bowls.

- Top each bowl with two basil leaves and add olive slice eyes. Spoon the cream cheese into a piping bag and pipe on the pupils, then add hair, noses and mouths. Serve with grissini.

BRILLIANT BULL BUTTY

SERVES: 1

Preparation time: 10 minutes

2 slices white bread

3 lettuce leaves

1 slice honey-roast ham

3 slices salami

2 slices green olive

1 red pepper ring, cut into 3 pieces

2 tsp mayonnaise

2 slices black olive

1 slice rye bread

- Lay the bread on top of a lettuce-lined serving plate. Cover the join with a slice of ham and top with two slices of salami.

- Cut the third slice of salami into a tongue shape and position below the nose. Lay two green olive slices on top of the nose and add a red pepper 'ring'.

- Make two dollops of mayonnaise for the eyes and add black olive pupils.

- Cut the hair out of the rye bread with a star-shaped cutter, then cut two triangles for the ears. Complete the bullock with red pepper horns.

SMOKED SALMON SEDAN

MAKES: 2

Preparation time: 15 minutes

2 slices sourdough toast

2 tbsp cream cheese

4 slices smoked salmon

2 lettuce leaves

4 slices cucumber

4 slices crinkle-cut carrot

2 black olives stuffed with lemon

2 green olives stuffed with pimento

2 redcurrants

1 slice smoked cheese, quartered

2 spring onions (scallions)

- Spread the toast with cream and cheese and lay the smoked salmon on top. Trim the edges to fit the bread and incorporate the trimmings on top.

- Lay the lettuce leaves on two plates and top with the toast.

- Make the wheels from cucumber and carrot and add bodywork details with the olives, redcurrants and cheese.

- Cut the spring onions into sections and use to add the door trim, exhaust pipe and exhaust fumes.

GRILLED CHEESE GARDEN

SERVES: 2

Preparation time: 10 minutes
Cooking time: 8 minutes

2 slices white bread

2 slices Gruyère

2 large frankfurters

4 quail eggs

2 cooked green beans, halved

8 cooked baby broad beans

- Preheat the grill to medium, then toast the bread on one side. Turn the bread over, top with cheese and toast until the toast is golden and the cheese has melted.

- Meanwhile, cut each frankfurter into 12 slices. Put four metal ring moulds in a large non-stick frying pan and set over a medium heat. Arrange six sausage slices round the inside edge of each mould and crack the eggs into the centres. Fry for 3 minutes or until the whites have set.

- Unmould the frankfurter flowers and lay two on top of each slice of cheese on toast. Add green bean stems and broad bean leaves.

MUNCHY MOUSE BAPS

SERVES: 4

Preparation time: 20 minutes

4 sesame baps

2 tbsp mayonnaise

8 lettuce leaves

4 slices cheese

12 slices salami

4 tomatoes, 2 sliced and 2 halved

4 slices ham

4 black olives

8 green olives

- Cut the baps in half horizontally and spread them with mayonnaise.

- Top each base with a lettuce leaf, a slice of cheese, three slices of salami and some of the sliced tomato.

- Use a round cookie cutter to cut two circles out of each slice of ham and use for the ears, making holes in the top of the baps with a knife.

- Slice the black olives and fit a small piece into the green olive holes to form the eyes. Use the halved tomatoes for the noses, topping each one with a piece of black olive.

- Use the rest of the lettuce leaves to garnish four plates before transferring the baps.

DINNER

SPOOKY SPAGHETTI

SERVES: 4

Preparation time: 15 minutes
Cooking time: 35 minutes

2 tbsp olive oil

1 onion, chopped

2 cloves of garlic, crushed

400 g / 14 oz / 2 cups canned tomatoes, chopped

400 g / 14 oz dried spaghetti

9 slices Provolone cheese

½ red pepper

12 black olives

- Heat the oil in a saucepan and fry the onion over a medium-low heat for 10 minutes or until softened. Add the garlic and stir for 2 more minutes.

- Pour in the chopped tomatoes, then half-fill the can with water and add it to the pan. Simmer the sauce for 20 minutes, then season to taste with salt and black pepper.

- Meanwhile, cook the spaghetti according to the packet instructions until al dente. Drain and divide between four plates then top with the sauce.

- Cut one of the Provolone slices into twelve thin wedges and use them for the fangs. Use the other whole slices for the eyes.

- Cut eight circles out of the red pepper for the irises, then slice the rest into thin strips to add the blood-shot detail.

- Slice the black olives and arrange the pieces to make the spiders, moustaches, eyebrows and pupils.

STUFFED MUSHROOM SNAILS

SERVES: 4

Preparation time: 15 minutes
Cooking time: 25 minutes

4 portobello mushrooms,
stalks removed

2 rashers streaky bacon, chopped

150 g / 5 ½ oz / 1 ½ cups Cheddar
cheese, grated

2 tbsp crème fraiche

175 g / 6 oz / 1 ½ cups
crinkle-cut carrots

300 g / 10 ½ oz / 2 cups frozen peas

8 cherry tomatoes

olives, green beans and sweetcorn
for the faces and bugs

- Preheat the oven to 180°C (160°C fan) / 350F / gas 4.

- Mix the bacon with the cheese and crème fraiche. Use the mixture to stuff the mushrooms, then roast them on a baking tray for 25 minutes or until tender to the point of a knife.

- Meanwhile, cook the carrots and peas for 4 minutes in two pans of boiling water. Drain well.

- Divide the peas between four warm plates to make the snails' bodies and position the mushrooms on top. Add detail to the shells with the carrots, reserving four slices for the faces.

- Add cherry tomato eyes to the snails, then complete the rest of the details with olives and green beans. Create a bug for each plate from olives, sweetcorn and peas.

DELICIOUS DINNER TRAIN

SERVES: 2

Preparation time: 20 minutes
Cooking time: 1 hour

4 medium baking potatoes

10 baby sweetcorn, halved lengthways

150 g / 5 ½ oz / 1 cup mixed frozen vegetables

24 crinkle-cut carrot slices

1 tbsp butter

2 spring onions (scallions), quartered lengthways

8 cm / 3 in garlic sausage, halved

2 small squares ham

1 black olive, halved

curly parsley, to garnish

- Preheat the oven to 220°C (200°C fan) / 425F / gas 7.

- Bake the potatoes for 1 hour, turning halfway through.

- Cook the mixed vegetables, sweetcorn and carrot slices in boiling water for 4 minutes, then drain well.

- Cut two of the potatoes in half and remove the skins. Carefully hollow out the centres with a teaspoon and set aside for the carriages. Skin the other two potatoes and carve them to resemble engines. Mash the off-cuts with the butter and set aside.

- Arrange the baby sweetcorn and spring onions on two warm plates to make the track and sit the potato engine and carriages on top. Set aside two pieces of green bean then fill the carriages with vegetables. Use carrot slices for the wheels, attaching each one with a little mashed potato.

- Complete the engines with the garlic sausage, ham, olive and green beans, using mashed potato as glue. Garnish with parsley and serve.

TOM CAT TOMATO RISOTTO

SERVES: 2

Preparation time: 20 minutes
Cooking time: 35 minutes

2 tbsp olive oil

1 onion, finely chopped

2 cloves of garlic, crushed

150 g / 5 ½ oz / 3/4 cup risotto rice

1 litre / 1 pint 15 fl. oz / 4 cups hot vegetable stock

250 ml / 9 fl. oz / 1 cup tomato passata

1 tbsp butter

50 g / 1 ¾ oz / 0.5 cup Parmesan, finely grated

cooked sliced beetroot and carrot for the hat

smoked cheese and garlic sausage for the ears, muzzle and collar

olives, tomatoes and sweetcorn for the eyes, mouth and flower

chives for the whiskers

- Heat the olive oil in a sauté pan and gently fry the onion for 5 minutes without colouring. Add the garlic and cook for 2 minutes then stir in the rice. When it is well coated with the oil, add two ladles of the hot stock.

- Cook, stirring occasionally, until most of the stock has been absorbed before adding the next two ladles. Continue in this way for around 20 minutes or until the rice is just tender, then season with salt and pepper.

- Set aside two large spoonfuls of rice, then stir the passata, butter and Parmesan into the pan. Turn off the heat, cover the pan and leave to stand for 5 minutes.

- Divide the risotto between four warm plates and shape each one into a cat's head. Spoon the plain rice into the centre of each face then make the hats from beetroot and carrot.

- Add a smoked cheese muzzle and collar to each cat and garlic sausage ears. Make the rest of the features from olives, tomatoes and sweetcorn before adding chive whiskers.

FRIENDLY FISH CAKES

SERVES: 4

Preparation time: 1 hour 30 minutes
Cooking time: 8 minutes

200 g / 7 oz / 1 ¼ cup skinless cod fillet, chopped

200 g / 7 oz / 1 ¼ cup skinless salmon fillet, chopped

2 tsp Dijon mustard

2 tbsp fresh dill, finely chopped

450 g / 1 lb / 2 cups leftover mashed potato

75 g / 2 ½ oz / ½ cup plain (all purpose) flour

2 eggs, beaten

150 g / 5 ½ oz / 1 cup fine dry breadcrumbs

sunflower oil for deep-frying

½ broccoli, cut into small florets

200 g / 7 oz / 1 cup canned sweetcorn

100 g / 3 ½ oz / 2/3 cup frozen peas, defrosted

2 small carrot slices

a small bunch chives

- Put the cod, salmon, mustard and dill in a food processor with a pinch of salt and pepper and pulse until finely chopped. Add the mashed potato and pulse until the mixture comes together into a ball. Use a fish-shaped cookie cutter to help you shape the mixture into eight fish, then chill in the fridge for 1 hour.

- Heat the oil in a deep fat fryer, according to the manufacturer's instructions, to a temperature of 180ºC / 350F. Put the flour, egg and breadcrumbs in three separate bowls. Dip the fish cakes alternately in the flour, egg and breadcrumbs.

- Lower the fish cakes in the fryer basket and cook for 8 minutes or until crisp and golden brown. Transfer to a kitchen paper lined bowl to remove any excess oil.

- While the fishcakes are cooking, blanch the vegetables and chives in boiling salted water, then drain well.

- Arrange the chives on four plates to look like seaweed and make the sea bed from sweetcorn, peas and broccoli. Lay the fish cakes on top and add carrot eyes and peas for the bubbles.

NATURE PASTA SCENE

SERVES: 2

Preparation time: 10 minutes
Cooking time: 12 minutes

200 g / 7 oz spaghetti

150 g / 5 ½ oz / 1 cup mixed
frozen vegetables

2 tbsp pesto

2 tbsp butter, melted

olives, chives and lambs
lettuce to garnish

- Cook the spaghetti in boiling salted water according to the
  packet instructions until al dente.

- Meanwhile, cook the vegetables in boiling water for 4
  minutes then drain well. Pick out the peas and arrange on
  two plates to make the dragonfly bodies, then make the
  heads, butterflies and flowers from pieces of carrot,
  sweetcorn, olives and chives.

- When the pasta is ready, drain it well and toss with the
  pesto, butter and the rest of the vegetables. Arrange on the
  plates, adding spaghetti wings to the dragonflies. Garnish
  with lambs lettuce.

HAPPY PIZZA FACES

MAKES: 4 SMALL PIZZAS

Preparation time: 2 hours 30 minutes
Cooking time: 10 minutes

200 g / 7 oz / 1 1/3 cups strong white bread flour

1/2 tsp easy blend dried yeast

75 ml / 2 1/2 fl. oz / 1/3 cup tomato pizza sauce

150 g / 5 1/2 oz / 1 1/2 cups mozzarella, grated

TO DECORATE:

2 tbsp fresh rosemary

8 slices black olive

2 cherry tomatoes

1 slice salami, halved

2 slices ham

1/4 yellow pepper

1/4 red pepper

2 slices green olive

- Mix together the flour and yeast. Stir into 140 ml of warm water to form a soft dough.

- Knead the dough on a lightly oiled surface for 10 minutes. Leave to rest for 1-2 hours until doubled in size.

- Preheat the oven to 220°C (200°C fan) / 425F / gas 7 and grease a non-stick baking tray.

- Knead the dough again then quarter it. Roll each piece into a circle, spread with pizza sauce and top with mozzarella.

- To make boy faces, arrange rosemary for hair and two slices of black olive for eyes. Add a cherry tomato nose and a salami smile.

- To make girl faces, use strips of ham for hair and make a pepper bow. Add red pepper smiles, green olive noses and black olive eyes.

- Drizzle the pizzas with olive oil and bake for 10 minutes or until the bases are cooked and crisp.

63

MOREISH MEATBALLS

SERVES: 4

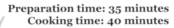

Preparation time: 35 minutes
Cooking time: 40 minutes

4 tbsp olive oil

1 onion, finely chopped

1 clove of garlic, crushed

250 g / 9 oz / 1 2/3 cups
minced beef

250 g / 9 oz / 1 2/3 cups
sausagemeat

50 g / 1 ¾ oz / 2/3 cup fresh
white breadcrumbs

1 egg yolk

300 g / 10 ½ oz / 2 cups crinkle-cut
carrot slices

6 frankfurters, 2 of them halved

100 g / 3 ½ oz / ¼ cup canned
sweetcorn

4 hard-boiled eggs, peeled
and halved

8 black olives, 4 of them halved

4 green olives, halved

1 bunch chives

- Preheat the oven to 190°C (170°C fan) / 375F / gas 5.

- Heat half the oil in an oven-proof frying pan and fry the onion for 5 minutes or until softened. Add the garlic and cook for 2 more minutes, stirring constantly, then scrape the mixture into a mixing bowl and leave to cool.

- Add the mince, sausagemeat, breadcrumbs and egg yolk. Mix well and season with salt and pepper, then shape into 12 meatballs.

- Heat the rest of the oil in the frying pan and sear the meatballs on all sides. Transfer to the oven and bake for 20 minutes or until cooked through.

- Meanwhile, cook the carrots in simmering water for 5 minutes. Add the frankfurters and sweetcorn to the pan, turn off the heat and leave to warm through for 5 minutes.

- When the meatballs are ready, arrange three on each plate and surround with a mane of carrots. Make each mouth from one and a half frankfurters, using sweetcorn for teeth.

- Use the eggs, olives and chives for the eyes, noses, ears and whiskers.

SAUSAGE & MASH MATES

SERVES: 4

Preparation time: 15 minutes
Cooking time: 25 minutes

900 g / 2 lb potatoes, peeled
and cubed

150 g / 5 ½ oz / 2/3 cup
butter, cubed

250 ml / 9 fl. oz / 1 cup milk, whole

16 cocktail sausages

400 g / 14 oz / 2 cups baked beans

- Cook the potatoes in boiling salted water for 12 minutes or until tender all the way through. Tip the potatoes into a colander and leave to drain.

- Put the saucepan back on the heat, add the butter and milk and bring to a simmer. Use a potato ricer to crush the potatoes straight into the hot milk, then briefly beat the mixture with a wooden spoon until smooth. Season to taste with salt and pepper and keep warm.

- Cook the sausages under a medium-hot grill for 10 minutes or until cooked-through, turning occasionally.

- Meanwhile, heat the beans in a saucepan until they start to simmer.

- Cover the bottom two thirds of four plates with mashed potato and spoon the beans into the top third to make the hair.

- Cut four of the sausages in half and position for the eyes, then use the rest to make noses and mouths.

BULL HEAD BOLOGNESE

SERVES: 6

Preparation time: 15 minutes
Cooking time: 1 hour 30 minutes

450 g / 1 lb / 3 cups minced beef

1 onion, finely chopped

1 carrot, half crinkle-cut,
half finely chopped

400 g / 14 oz / 2 cups canned
tomatoes, chopped

2 tbsp tomato puree

600 g / 14 oz dried spaghetti

300 g / 10 ½ oz / 2 cups peas,
defrosted if frozen

300 g / 10 ½ oz / 2 cups canned
sweetcorn, drained

12 okra

1 red pepper, cut into 6 pieces

12 spinach leaves

6 black olives, halved

- Brown the mince in a saucepan over a high heat and reserve. Fry the onion and chopped carrot over a medium-low heat for 10 minutes or until softened and sweet.

- Pour in the tomatoes, then half-fill the can with water and add it to the pan. Stir in the puree and return the mince. Cover and simmer for 1 hour, then season to taste.

- Cook the spaghetti according to the packet instructions until al dente. While the spaghetti is cooking, cook the peas, sweetcorn, okra and sliced carrot separately in boiling water for 4 minutes.

- Drain the spaghetti immediately. Use strands to make the outline of the faces on six warm plates, then arrange the rest on top.

- Fill in the outline of the faces with Bolognese, add a red pepper tongue, spinach ears, okra horns and carrot and olive eyes. Complete each plate with peas and sweetcorn.

GAMMON GALLEONS

SERVES: 4

**Preparation time: 10 minutes
Cooking time: 1 hour**

4 baking potatoes

1 large gammon steak

300 g / 10 ½ oz / 2 cups mixed
frozen vegetables

8 small knobs butter

½ lettuce, chopped

fish-shaped savoury
snacks to garnish

- Preheat the oven to 220°C (200°C fan) / 425F / gas 7.

- Bake the potatoes for 1 hour, turning halfway through.

- Towards the end of the cooking time, grill or fry the
  gammon steak for 2 minutes on each side. Cook the mixed
  vegetables in boiling water for 4 minutes, then drain well.

- Cut the potatoes in half and top each one with a knob of
  butter. Divide the lettuce between four plates and arrange
  the potatoes on top.

- Cut the gammon steak into eight wedges and use for the
  sails, attaching with cocktail sticks. Top the galleons with
  vegetables and garnish with fish-shaped savoury snacks.

DINNER

SCAMPI SALAD SNAILS

SERVES: 1

Preparation time: 15 minutes
Cooking time: 15 minutes

1 tbsp olive oil

1 tbsp white wine vinegar

½ tsp caster (superfine) sugar

¼ cucumber, thinly sliced

½ carrot, peeled and thinly sliced

5 breaded wholetail scampi

4 little gem lettuce leaves

1 cherry tomato

1 chive

¼ tsp mayonnaise

- Mix together the oil, vinegar and sugar to make a dressing and season with salt and pepper. Toss with the cucumber and carrot and set aside to macerate.

- Cook the scampi according to the packet instructions until piping hot throughout.

- Arrange the carrot and cucumber slices on a plate to make the snail's shell and create a bed of lettuce for it to lie on.

- Position the scampi to form the body and make a head out of the tomato and chives. Add tiny blobs of mayonnaise to make the eyes.

MAC & CHEESE CHUMS

SERVES: 4

Preparation time: 15 minutes
Cooking time: 35 minutes

400 g / 14 oz / 4 cups dried macaroni

2 tbsp butter

1 leek, sliced

4 rashers streaky bacon, chopped

2 tbsp plain (all-purpose) flour

600 ml / 1 pint / 2 ½ cups milk, whole

150 g / 5 ½ oz / 1 ½ cups Cheddar cheese, grated

8 frozen peas, defrosted

2 baby sweetcorn, halved lengthways

1 tomato, seeded and cut into 8 wedges

a variety of herbs and vegetables to complete the faces

- Preheat the oven to 180°C (160°C fan) / 350F / gas 4. Cook the macaroni in boiling, salted water for 10 minutes or until almost cooked. Drain well.

- Meanwhile, melt the butter in a medium saucepan. Reserve eight slices of leek for the eyes then fry the rest with the bacon for 5 minutes.

- Stir in the flour, then gradually whisk in the milk until it is all incorporated. Cook the sauce over a low heat, stirring constantly, until the mixture is thick and consistent.

- Take the pan off the heat and stir in half of the cheese and the macaroni. Season to taste, then divide between four individual baking dishes.

- Sprinkle over the remaining cheese then bake for 25 minutes until the golden brown and cooked through.

- Arrange the leek slices and peas on top for the eyes and add sweetcorn noses. Use tomato slices for the lips, then get creative and complete the faces with herbs and vegetables.

71

SLY SPAGHETTI FOX

SERVES: 4

Preparation time: 20 minutes
Cooking time: 35 minutes

2 tbsp olive oil

1 red pepper, finely chopped

2 cloves of garlic, crushed

400 g / 14 oz / 2 cups canned tomatoes, chopped

1 tbsp tomato puree

1 tsp dried oregano

400 g / 14 oz dried spaghetti

4 slices Emmental

4 black olives

8 slices carrot

- Heat the oil in a saucepan and fry the red pepper over a medium-low heat for 10 minutes or until softened and sweet. Add the garlic and stir for 2 more minutes.

- Pour in the chopped tomatoes, then half-fill the can with water and add it to the pan with the tomato puree and dried oregano. Simmer the sauce for 20 minutes, then blend until smooth in a liquidiser. Season with salt and pepper.

- Meanwhile, cook the spaghetti according to the packet instructions until al dente. Drain well.

- Reserve a small amount of sauce for the ears and stir the rest into the spaghetti to coat. Divide between four warm plates and shape into a fox. Arrange small pieces of spaghetti to make the outline of the ears and fill in with the reserved sauce.

- Cut the Emmental to make the eyes and arrange the rest on the plate next to each fox.

- Cut the olives into small pieces to make the eyes, nose and whiskers and add carrots for paws.

SNACKS & DESSERTS

PIGS IN BANDAGES

MAKES: 8

Preparation time: 20 minutes
Cooking time: 20 minutes

2 sheets ready-rolled puff pastry

1 large egg, beaten

8 chipolata sausages

1 tbsp American mustard

- Preheat the oven to 220°C (200°C fan) / 425F / gas 7 and line a baking tray with baking parchment.

- Brush the pastry sheets with egg then cut them into 1 cm wide strips. Wrap the strips around the sausages, leaving a small space for the 'faces'.

- Transfer the sausages to the prepared baking tray and brush with more beaten egg. Bake for 20 minutes or until the pastry is golden brown on top and crisp underneath and the sausages are cooked through.

- Use a squeezy bottle or piping bag to pipe the mustard 'eyes' onto the mummies.

LADYBIRD BISCUITS

MAKES: 6

Preparation time: 10 minutes

6 oatcakes

50 g / 1 ¾ oz / ¼ cup cream cheese

3 small tomatoes, quartered

4 black olives

3 garlic chives, chopped

- Spread the oatcakes with cream cheese and top each one with two tomato wedges.

- Chop two of the olives into small pieces to use for the spots and cut the rest in half for the heads.

- Insert two pieces of chive into each olive head for the antennae and sprinkle the rest over the top.

SCRUMPTIOUS SPIDERS

SERVES: 4

Preparation time: 10 minutes

4 apricots

12 strawberries, hulled and halved

2 red grapes, sliced

2 tbsp blackcurrant jam (jelly)

- Cut the apricots in half and remove the stones. Reassemble the apricots, slightly off-set, and transfer to four plates.

- Arrange six strawberry halves around the edge of each apricot, then stick two slices of grape onto each spider with a dab of blackcurrant jam.

- Pick eight blackcurrants out of the jam and use them for the centre of the eyes.

MUMMIFIED PEPPERS

MAKES: 6

Preparation time: 30 minutes
Cooking time: 25 minutes

3 pale green peppers

4 merguez sausages, skinned

2 tbsp red pesto

2 sheets filo pastry

75 g / 2 ½ oz / 1/3 cup butter, melted

12 candy eyeballs

- Preheat the oven to 200°C (180°C fan) / 400F / gas 6.

- Cut the peppers in half through the stalk and remove the seeds and inner membrane.

- Mix the sausagemeat with the pesto and stuff it inside the peppers.

- Brush the filo sheets with melted butter, then cut them into very thin ribbons and wrap them round and round the peppers to form the bandages.

- Transfer the peppers to a baking tray and brush any remaining butter over the top. Bake the peppers for 25 minutes or until golden brown on top and cooked through.

- Arrange the candy eyeballs on top and serve immediately.

Funny Clown Crackers

MAKES: 8 CLOWNS

Preparation time: 20 minutes

8 cream crackers

2 tbsp cream cheese

12 flat-leaf parsley leaves

4 slices cheese, halved

8 rosemary leaves

2 chives, cut into 1 cm pieces

8 redcurrants

2 tbsp sweet chilli (chili) sauce or tomato ketchup

- Spread the crackers with cream cheese and add two parsley leaves to each one to make the hair.

- Cut each piece of cheese into a hat shape and position at the top of the crackers. Add a rosemary 'feather' to each hat.

- Make a cross out of two pieces of chive for each eye and use the redcurrants for the noses.

- Put the chilli sauce or ketchup into a squeezy bottle or small piping bag and pipe on the mouths and eyes, then add a small dot to the end of the rosemary feathers to keep them in place.

APPLE PIE CONES

SERVES: 8

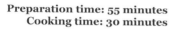

Preparation time: 55 minutes
Cooking time: 30 minutes

400 g / 14 oz / 2 2/3 cups plain (all purpose) flour

50 g / 1 ¾ oz / 0.5 cup icing (confectioners') sugar

200 g / 7 oz / 3/4 cup butter, cubed

1 kg / 2 lb 3 oz bramley apples; peeled, cored and chopped

125 g / 4 ½ oz / ½ cup caster (superfine) sugar

1 egg, beaten

8 bananas, sliced

8 cherries

- Mix the flour and icing sugar together, then rub in the butter until it resembles breadcrumbs. Add just enough cold water to bring the mixture together into a dough, then wrap in clingfilm and chill for 30 minutes.

- Meanwhile, put the apples and caster sugar in a saucepan with a splash of water. Cover and cook for 10 minutes, stirring occasionally, until the apples start to break down. Leave to cool.

- Preheat the oven to 190°C (170° fan) / 375F / gas 5. Roll out two thirds of the pastry on a lightly floured surface and use it to line a large pie tin. Spoon in the apple.

- Roll out the reserved pastry and roll a lattice cutter over the top. Gently ease the pastry apart to show the holes, then transfer it to the top of the pie and secure with a dab of water. Trim the edges and brush the top with beaten egg.

- Bake the pie for 30 minutes or until crisp underneath. Cut the pie into eight wedges and transfer to eight plates.

- Arrange the sliced bananas to look like ice cream and top each one with a cherry.

RICE PUDDING PIRATES

SERVES: 4

Preparation time: 15 minutes
Cooking time: 1 hour 30 minutes

110 g / 4 oz / 1/2 cup short
grain rice

1 tsp ground cinnamon

75 g / 2 ½ oz / 1/3 cup caster
(superfine) sugar

1.2 litres / 2 pints / 4 ½ cups
milk, whole

4 pieces fruit leather (fruit rolls)

8 canned prunes

4 blueberries

• Preheat the oven to 140°C (120°C fan) / 275F / gas 1.

• Stir the rice, cinnamon and sugar into the milk in a baking
dish, then cover and bake for 1 hour 30 minutes.

• While the rice is cooking, cut the fruit leather into four
eye-patch shapes.

• Discard the skin on top of the pudding and give it a stir,
then spoon into four bowls. Top each one with a prune
moustache, a blueberry eye and a fruit leather eye-patch.

HAPPY APPLE ALIENS

MAKES: 6

Preparation time: 15 minutes

1 Granny Smith apple

100 g / 3 ½ oz / ½ cup smooth peanut butter

6 slices strawberry

50 g / 1 ¾ oz / ½ cup sunflower seeds

10 candy eyeballs

- Cut the apple into 6 wedges and remove the core from each one. Cut a small wedge out of the back of each apple and spread them with peanut butter.

- Add a strawberry slice to each 'mouth' for the tongue and insert sunflower seeds along the top edge for the teeth.

- Attach the candy eyeballs with a dab of peanut butter.

COWARDLY LION COOKIES

SERVES: 1

Preparation time: 20 minutes

1 fluted-edge waffle biscuit

1 butter galette

2 ginger nut biscuits

1 tbsp dulce de leche

2 amaretti biscuits

2 green sugar-coated chocolate sweets

black food colour pen

1 yellow sugar-coated chocolate sweet, halved

1 brown sugar-coated chocolate sweet

1 orange wine gum, halved

1 fizzy strawberry bootlace

1 red jelly sweet

- Arrange the waffle biscuit and butter galette on a plate to make the head and body of the lion. Lay a ginger nut on top of each, attaching with a dab of dulce de leche.

- Use more dulce de leche to glue the amaretti biscuits to the face, followed by green sweets for the eyes. Draw on pupils with the pen.

- Add yellow ears, a brown nose and wine gum feet, attaching with dulce de leche as before. Use the fizzy bootlace and jelly sweet to make the tail.

ZESTY ZEBRA

SERVES: 1

Preparation time: 20 minutes

1 banana, peeled

1 purple plum

1 black cherry, halved and stoned

½ red apple

2 small squares green apple

1 red grape, halved

- Cut one third off the end of the banana, then cut two thin slices and reserve. Arrange the two large pieces of banana so that they form the body and head of the zebra.

- Use a vegetable peeler to pare the skin from the plum, then cut it into thin strips with a sharp knife. Smooth the strips across the banana to make stripes.

- Cut the top edge off the reserved banana slices and use them for the eyes, adding black cherry pupils.

- Cut a slice from the cut side of the apple, then cut four thin strips for the legs and use an outer strip for the tail. Cut two wedges out of the rest of the apple half and reserve one of them. Use the rest as the zebra's muzzle, sliding it under the banana. Use the reserved apple wedge for the ears.

- Complete the zebra's face with green apple teeth and a red grape nose.

FRUITY FISH BOWL

SERVES: 1

Preparation time: 5 minutes

2 thick slices orange

4 dried apricots

1 slice red apple

2 currants

50 g / 1 ¾ oz / 1/3 cup blueberries

- Lay the orange slices on a plate and arrange the apricots to make the fish tails.

- Cut two small circles from the apple slice to make the eyes and use currants for the pupils. Cut four small pieces of apple skin to make the mouths.

- Use six of the blueberries for the bubbles and arrange the rest at the bottom of the plate.

Teacake Teddy Bear

SERVES: 1

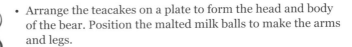

Preparation time: 15 minutes

2 chocolate marshmallow teacakes

4 malted milk balls

2 brown sugar-coated chocolate sweets

6 yellow sugar-coated chocolate sweets

1 red fruit gum

1 fizzy strawberry bootlace

blue and brown royal icing

2 yellow bean-shaped sweets

- Arrange the teacakes on a plate to form the head and body of the bear. Position the malted milk balls to make the arms and legs.

- Use brown sugar-coated chocolate sweets for the ears and use two yellow ones for the eyes. Add a fruit gum nose and a bootlace smile, then pipe the pupils onto the eyes with a little blue royal icing.

- Make the bees' wings from the rest of the yellow sugar-coated chocolate sweets, adding bean-shaped sweet bodies. Pipe the stripes and heads on with brown royal icing.

INDEX

INDEX

Picture Credits:
  16, 19, 20, 25, 35, 37, 60, 68, 70, 74, 76, 79, 81 © Alamy

  33, 44, 66, 71 © Getty Images

  40, 41, 48, 56, 57, 62, 65, 67, 80, 89, 90, 93 © Good Mood Edition GmbH

  All other images: © iStock